DAUGHTERS

OF

BASTARDS

By

Iris Berry

Punk ⚡ Hostage ⚡ Press

The Daughters of Bastards
Copyright © Iris Berry 2012
An imprint of Punk Hostage Press

ISBN 978-0-9851293-2-3

Punk Hostage Press
Hollywood, California
www.punkhostagepress.com

Editor
A. Razor

Associate Editors:
Michele McDannold
Gwenn Morreale

Introduction
Pleasant Gehman

Forward
Dimitri Monroe

Cover Design
Geoff Melville

Back Cover Photo
Christopher Martin

Editor's Acknowledgements

This book is a real labor of love, as most books are, but it also represents a special friendship and partnership that has been at the foundation of the press that this book is published on.

Iris Berry has been writing, editing and publishing works from her mind and her heart since the early 1980s. Her work has been inspirational and historical all at once. The words here tell the story of that beginning and that progression through some of the wildest of times during one of the most unique eras that Los Angeles has ever known. It also tells the story of a young woman coming of age in the sex, drugs and rock 'n' roll inspired madness of those times. A woman who bears a shared first hand witness to her own incredible survival.

Editing together these pages has been a task that many have supported with hard work and heartfelt anticipation. It is an effort that has been influenced by the ghosts of the past that are memorialized by her words. It is an effort that has been influenced by all those that have been there for Iris along the way, with encouragement and support when she needed it most. It is an effort that creates new relationships that moves the story forward even farther into the promising future.

Many thanks to Pleasant Gehman and Dimitri Monroe for providing such a richly textured introduction and foreword to the book, as well as Gwenn Morreale for her support with the editorial process, and Michele McDannold for her much needed support proof reading, and all around enthusiasm for the press. Thank you so much to Geoff Melville for the cover design that gives homage to the John Martin, Black Sparrow Press influence on our work. We also give a hearty thank you to Lee McGrevin for all the technical support and hard work he has done for the press in general, and for his loyal friendship. Thanks also for Christopher Martin and the inspiring back cover photo of Iris at the Beat Motel in Desert Hot Springs California.

A big, posthumous thank you for the enigmatic Sholom "Red" Stodolsky and his Baroque Books at 1643 N. Las Palmas Ave. in Hollywood, California. Which was the place both author and editor first engaged the literary presence of independently published books that impact the world by surviving no matter what.

Also, for the writer, her relationship with Marc Rude, whose art and life was a part of hers for so long it will never be forgotten.

Sadly, the recently departed Scott Wannberg for the years of soulful laughter and wordful inspiration that will never fade away, as well as the kindness of Mike Taylor who was so supportive of our work before he also passed away last year.

We also need to thank Beyond Baroque Literary Arts Center in Venice, California for all they have done to help us in our efforts and the role they play in supporting so many important literary voices from Los Angeles and beyond.

Special thank yous to S.A. Griffin for his profound friendship, to our community of friends and writers that are a big part of what we do and all that we will be doing in the future, such as A.D. Winans, Alex Bacon, Alexandra Naughton, Alicia Young, Amelie Frank, Annette Cruz, Art Kunkin R.I.P., Bill Gainer, Bucky Sinister, Chris D., C.V. Auchterlonie, Carl Schneider, Carlye Archibeque, Carolyn Srygley-Moore, Chris Bailey, David Matthew Koskoff (R.I.P.), Danny Garcia, Danny Baker, Dennis Cruz, Diana Rose, Dire McCain, Doug Knott, Felon O'Rielly, Frank Reardon, Fred Spigelman, Gil T., Ginger Coyote, Harvest House, Hollie Hardy, Hudson Marquez, Jack Grisham, Jack Shaw, Jack Varnell, James Anthony Tropeano III (R.I.P.), Jane Cantillon, Janet Cunningham, (R.I.P.), Jeannie Davis, Jennifer Joseph, Jim Lopez, Joe Donnelly, Joel Landmine, John Dorsey, Jon Hess, Keirda BahruthBallard, Lee Quarnstrom, Lola the cat, LuisJ.Rodriguez, Maharet Christina Hughes, Marc Savage, Maria Bermudez, Marina Lenter, Mark Hartenbach, Maxine Brumer, Michael C. Ford, Michael Juliani, Michael Marcus, Nadia Bruce-Rawlings, Nellie Lorenz, Nicholas Berry, Puma Perl, Ratsass Stratford, Rich Ferguson, Richard Modiano, Rick Ballard, Rick Lupert, Sammy "Town" McBride, SB Stokes, Sevie Bates, Sharon Virag, Sonny Giordano, Steve Abee, Stories Books and Cafe, Susan Clary, Susan Hayden, Teddy & Sage Quinn, Vicky Hamilton, Violet Liquori, Vivien Cooper, Wyatt Doyle, Wanda Coleman (R.I.P.) and Yvonne de La Vega.

All these people and so many more have inspired or supported or done both simultaneously so that we might be able to bring some more books into this world and be a part of a vibrant community of people who still believe and promote the words of writers, both written and spoken, so that those words may continue to give back what they will as the everlasting treasure that we know they are.

~ **A. Razor**   2012

Introduction

Iris Berry: writer, actress, pop culture historian…
a gilded glamazon whose chaotic romances and offhand
substance abuse could easily give Charles Bukowski -or
Erroll Flynn, for that matter- a run for their money. I know
this; I can vouch for her because I was there. In the book
you are now holding, The Daughters Of Bastards, it's all
set down in Iris' pure and honest prose, a real Hollywood
fairytale for the mind's eye, chronicling choice fragments
of her life- from the penthouses to the gutter - along the
Boulevard Of Broken Dreams.

What can I say about her or her writing that I haven't
said already? She writes her experiences with wit, grace
and deadly precision. Her lullaby-and-bedtime-story voice
is like a haunting tour of Los Angeles that lingers like one
of the city's famous unsolved murders. Her writing is
gritty and scarred, but loaded with details and an ironic,
wry sense of humor. Her words come from survivor's
wisdom, but always nourish a naïve sense of universal
hope. Telling stories of Hollywood as it is and was, with a
nonchalance that's fragile, intelligent and tough all at
once. She doesn't hide the often-unpleasant scenarios
beneath flowery language; everything you will read here
is true and unembellished, except by her gorgeous turns of
phrase.

We are both the Daughters Of Bastards… our fathers
probably would've been best friends had they known each
other. I can see them drinking, womanizing and making
up barely credible alibis together, but they never met.
Separately they produced two beautifully damaged

daughters that literally grew up together, too smart, too wounded and too ambitious for their own good.

We outlived our fathers and acted out their legacies, but both of us were able to step outside of ourselves, break the insane hereditary cycle, and put our misadventures into words ...because in order to make sense of things, we had to.

Iris is my sister, my twin soul, and my "other half": she might as well be my spouse. At this point in our lives, we're way beyond common-law. We've been through a lot together and I believe our unique relationship is the longest-running and most stable one in either of our lives. For years, Iris and I played in bands together, lived together and didn't pay the rent together; we played musical bar stools, worked side by side at bars and at handbag stores. We traded clothes, ideas, drugs, cocktails, bites of Top Ramen and boyfriends.

I was lucky enough to share most of the incidents detailed in this book with Iris... and as soon as you turn this page you can, too.

~ **Pleasant Gehman**   2012

Forward

Iris Berry and her spellbinding words o' wonder probably need little trumpeting amidst this drunken choir we got here, but for any of you strays, and stragglers, who've stumbled in late...She's a visitor of cool places, a medium of sorts, a watcher of the night, a capturer of bottled lightning. She communicates with the spirits, brings long darkened bar-rooms back to life, she sees the glitz in the gutter, she can even talk to drunk people. The sound of her smoldering voice is enough to get ya good 'n' swizzled.

Iris was born in L.A., because the gods understood: that city needed a heart. From Pink's hot dog stand, to the tavern where the Black Dahlia got sauced-up, from Arthur Lee's castle where Jim Morrison used to skinny dip, to the "Riot House", from the Tropicana, to the Sugar Shack, from Schwab's soda fountain to Canter's Deli, from the freakishly attired carpet-baggers of Topanga Canyon, to the aging songwriters who sit around their deteriorating mansions, drinking Port wine, in their underwear, in the various hidden nooks and cul de sacs of old Mt. Houdini. From Duke's to the Starwood, the Cathay de Grande, and Raji's, the Zero Zero Club, the Masque, and the Music Machine..

.In the days before the on-line surveillance grid, we used to follow her escapades in the pages of L.A. Weekly and in our dearly departed brethren, Shane Williams' always entertaining column in the much missed pages of "Flipside" magazine. Iris is a real smoke-catcher. Her sultry prose can transport you back to all these spots, allowing one to glimpse the flashing lights of long faded moments in time. Under shadows of palm trees, where surgically-enhanced relatives of rich people become celebrities, for doing nothing but lounging beside dirty swimming pools, and vacantly shopping on Melrose Avenue, while irreplaceable geniuses die in the gutter, forgotten, and alone.

The Hollywood underground? Iris Berry wrote the book on it. Pioneer, Poet, Pin-up, Punk, spoken word artist, film actress, community organizer, bartending confidante to all the original L.A. Stars of goth and cow-punk, along with an admiring retinue of old Hollywood industry types who hounded our heroine for dates, and were still prone to calling the well-bourbon "brown plaid".

Intellectual bombshell, video vixen, chap-book barterer, legendary Tinsel-Town temptress, Hollyweird historian, habitué of Disgraceland, Iris has to be one of the most kickass dames on the globe. Humanitarian. Empath. Author, archivist. Vocalist of the Lame Flames, Ringling Sisters, and many, many more. She was the sultry star of the Little King's video for "Dirty Pool", appears in Dramarama's "Haven't Got A Clue" vid, made cameos in many others. Horror star. Nurturer of agonized brilliance.

A mutha of mercy, Iris can hear the truth, inside the lies...Her long enduring, richly detailed poems and prose bleed pure compassion, and never mind giving you quarters for the cigarette machine-with an eagle eye for nuanced details, callously overlooked by lesser scribes, and corporate-hack screenwriters. A dynamo, intuitive scene queen, always on the pulse beat, never failing to recognize a fleeting sunset, genuine article talent,

12

shimmery phrase, sugary melody, or exceptional character.

I never understood how she maintained her sincerity amidst all that spray tanned hustling. Fame is mostly something that horrible people have to purchase for their obnoxious kids, in this country. Iris was focused on doing her work, conveying painful truths, and witnessing ephemeral beauty. She sees the subtleties beyond the surfaces, transcends the cliche's, outlived the odds.

An outsider's insider, in the tradition of the sixties beats, desert novelists, the old soul hellions of post-punk, and finger poppin' hep cats that time forgot. Names like Nathaniel West, George Higgins, Denis Johnson, Hunter S. Thompson, Mary Gaitskill, John Fante, Malcolm Lowery, Henry Miller, Raymond Carver. Old Hollywood, wise guys and showgirls, surfboards and Gidget bikinis, safety pinned cheeks and rhinestone sunglasses, souvenir maracas and corny postcards, dune-buggies and swanky pink Cadillacs, shit-faced pianos, perennial bohemia. The death rock kids, the Mau-Maus, and "Miki Dora Lives!" I envy her abilities, but admire her boundless courage and generosity of soul.

She's befriended many maniacs, throughout the years. Fortune Tellers and derelicts. Rock stars and bank robbers. Bone jewelry makers and errant glamour dolls...Grieving, heartsick men with missing teeth and lopsided fedoras. Winos who talked like be bop detectives...Few, who ever shone pure white light, as moon-silvery as the true queen of luscious language and literary luminosity. The Barbarella of Beat. The High-Priestess Of Hip, El Lay's own, Iris Berry...Dig it!

~ **Dimitri Monro**e, Outlaw Singer   2012

This book is dedicated to…

All the mothers and daughters with no place to go.
To my mother, may she rest in peace, for making sure she
and her four children did have a place to go.
And for so much more.

To my father, may he rest in peace, for teaching me about
real life and keeping me safe.
To my entire family and my nearest and dearest friends
who always make this crazy ride make sense.

To Dave Alvin and my dearest friend and other half,
Pleasant Gehman for -Once Upon A Time-forcing me to
take my words out of my bedroom and into the world; to
A. Razor, also, for continuing to carry that torch along
with his great vision, deep devotion to literature and
priceless friendship.

To Beyond Baroque Literary Arts Center in Venice
Beach, California, for providing a space for writers to
flourish and for being a source of positive relationships
and inspirations for so many years.

And last, but certainly not least, this book is dedicated to
Red Stodolsky for providing myself and many others with
an irreplaceable literary education.

~ Iris Berry 2012

"Buy the Ticket, Take the Ride."

~ Hunter S. Thompson

As Good as It Gets

In the past few years
I've learned
that just because you're
loyal
honest
and devoted
does not mean
it will be reciprocated
that sometimes
sadly
no good deed
goes unpunished
and most movies
do not resemble
real life
especially the ones
with the big budgets
and what my grandmothers
told me about men
is true
I've also learned
that no matter how much
you know and love somebody
they can still have secrets
that could break your heart
and possibly kill you
I've also learned
don't rely on fortune cookies
but never let

a good wishbone
go to waste
that nothing is personal
and everything is personal
no one is perfect
especially me
and the more mistakes
I make
the more human and nice
I am towards you
and the more powerful
I think
I am
the more danger
I am in
I've learned
that everyone dies
some quickly
some slowly
so it's best
to live
the life
you really want
It's taken me forever
to realize
that I still haven't
grown-up
and that
somehow
I still
have the fantasy

that as long
as I am
a good person
life will get better
but what I've really learned is
the clock is tick tick ticking
and maybe
I should
do my best
to leave this place
with a smile on my face
and love in my heart
for you
and for me
and maybe that's
as good
as it gets
and if that's the case
I will
consider myself
lucky…

The Pink Mansion

In 1982 the streets of Hollywood were vacant and barren, a ghost town, like the abandoned movie set that it was. No tourists, no glamour. Just a has-been stretch of a boulevard with tarnished and littered stars on a sidewalk of Babylon dreams. Inhabited by the homeless left over Hollywood hopefuls, pushing shopping carts, talking about Frank Sinatra and Lana Turner, still waiting to get discovered. And a bunch of us punk rock kids from broken homes, or no homes, trying to figure it all out, running wild in the abandoned streets and having the time of our lives. It felt very pre-apocalyptic. We were all waiting for the world to end in 1984. With two years left to go, there was no time to waste.

The world did end in 1984, but not in the way Orwell predicted, he was a few decades off. It ended for us in Los Angeles by having the 1984 Olympics here. People from all over the world attended the festivities and realized all the opportunity, a whole new kind of gold rush. They came back and turned Los Angeles into a city that I no longer recognize...no longer the city where I could feel the majestic spirits of so many Eras. The 1970s and the politically, rebellious, rock 'n' roll 1960s on the

25

Sunset Strip, or the glamour and corruption of the 1950s, and the roar of the 'New Hollywood' in the 1920s on Hollywood Boulevard. Even though Hollywood was abandoned in 1982, there were still left over remnants from the celebrations. All the old ghosts and some of the old haunts were still here. And I was in love with it all...

* * *

Hollywood, Ca. January 1982...

From the minute I heard about the Zero Zero, I was intrigued. And once I got inside, I was hooked. A Hollywood underground afterhours club. If you didn't know it was there, you didn't know it was there. And if you wanted to get in, you had to know somebody. Being young and female, got me in, no problem.

It was tucked away in an unmarked storefront in the shadow of the Capitol Records building on a lonely strip of Cahuenga Boulevard, just off the 101 Freeway, as it spilled into Hollywood heading south from the San Fernando Valley.

Carlos Guitarlos, from the band, Top Jimmy and the Rhythm Pigs, worked the door. If he didn't know you or like you, you weren't getting in.

Because of the no selling liquor after 2 am law, the loophole was a, "suggested" five-dollar donation at the door that got you all the free plain wrap beer and boxed wine you could drink before the sun came up or the police bust in, which ever came first.

Top Jimmy worked the bar. Jimmy was the perfect bartender, a drunk and sassy white boy, blues singer, always good for a one-liner, delivered with a whiskey soaked, southern drawl.

Hidden under the bar was a jug of Plain Wrap vodka and a jug of Plain Wrap whiskey, for the VIPs, like David Lee Roth, who eventually became a not so silent, silent owner.

The jukebox had it all, but nothing you'd ever hear on any commercial radio station—a wide range—spanning from Robert Johnson, Chet Baker, Art Pepper, John Lee Hooker, Dave Brubeck, Santo and Johnny, Screamin Jay Hawkins, Jimmy Cliff...to X, The Blasters, The Cramps, The Plugz, The Weirdos and Fear. It opened every Friday and Saturday night at 2 a.m. A good place to get booze and a buzz, while the rest of the city was asleep, or doing whatever people in the underbelly do...

During the day it functioned as an art gallery. Displaying artists; Robert Williams, Jules Bates, Raymond Pettibone, Georganne Deen and Big Daddy Ed Roth, to name a few. Many Lowbrow artists before the term existed. At night the place was always packed with a varied crowd, existing solely as a hideaway for underground artists and punk rock luminaries whose 45s were on heavy rotation on the jukebox. Musicians, intellectuals, art school escapes, punk rockers, drug dealers, porn stars, strippers, mainstream and underground film makers, actors and directors. It always felt like how New Years Eve was supposed to feel. Everyone laughing and dancing, drinking, smoking pot and snorting coke, all out in the open. It was a cross between the party scene in Breakfast At Tiffany's meets Repo Man.

I finally found a place where I felt at home. Being from the San Fernando Valley where all the clubs were Disco, filled with blow dried, blow snorting, Valley boys who drove convertible Porsche 914s, and Valley girls in satin shorts, Chemin De Fer and Ditto Jeans, six inch platform Candies and tube tops, all trying to get into those convertible Porsche 914s, (the kind of people they make Reality TV shows about these days, 35 years later). But not at the Zero Zero, Clandestine and forbidden, no one went there to be seen, it was a hideaway, which is exactly why we were there, we were getting away with something.

I got a job there during the day minding the art gallery—for the curious who couldn't get in at night—to check the place out, and hopefully, buy some Art. The perfect job, I was selling pot and Quaaludes on the side, so the fact that it didn't pay much didn't matter, it was a good place to supplement my income. I had a 1974, gold Volkswagen Beetle. The trunk in the front was always a bitch to get open. On one particularly hot sweltering day I was trying to get it open, but getting nowhere, a couple of guys walked by. "Ah, some brut strength," shouting to them, "Hey, can you guys give me a hand?" One of them started clapping his hands. "Ha ha, very fucking funny." If I didn't have customers waiting, I might have thought it was funny.

There have been moments and snapshots of time in my life that have been pivotal, radically changing the course of everything, and this was one of them.

The guy clapping his hands was Justin Luck, and his friend was called Animal. Animal had a shaved head with a chainsaw tattooed on it, and Justin had a full head of hair, kind of rockabilly, but didn't really make a strong commitment, just a one style suits all kind of deal. When they got the trunk open, there was about 10 bags of weed and a few clear, zip lock bags filled with Quaaludes. They were immediately my new best friends and followed me back into the gallery. Animal eventually got board—three's company—it was obvious that Justin and I were hitting it off. Justin was charming and funny and was not one to pass up a good thing. When I brought him back to my house, he realized, even more, what a "good thing" I was.

I lived on Highland Avenue and 3rd Street, just north of Wilshire Boulevard near the Miracle Mile District. In a pink, two-story, Spanish Villa style mansion in Hancock Park, where all the old Hollywood money still lived. It wasn't your typical L.A. old-money mansion—it was faded, neglected and overgrown. The first time I went there was to see a co-worker's band rehearse. I was temping at CBS Records in Century City, and Bethany who sat at the desk next to me, invited me to check out her band. I parked on Highland Avenue, right in front of the house and managed to get through the overgrown ivy that buried the front porch. On the front door was a vintage door knocker, with a brass lion's head that stared back at me. I would later discover how an item so small, could be so loud, echoing throughout the house, and brutal on a hangover.

The first thing I noticed upon entry was the caramel hardwood floors and matching spiral staircase in the foyer, such a grand entrance, right out of an old Hollywood movie. At closer inspection, I was shocked to find the house completely empty, every room, stark naked, not even a kitchen table, vacant bookshelves and blank walls. The only visible items that inhabited the house were a varied collection of musical equipment in the library and a futon bed. If I was a detective, I would have immediately assumed something fishy was going on here. Mathew, the owner, inherited the mansion from his parents. The slightest mention or inquiry of them and Mathew's demeanor changed dramatically, his disdain for his parents was obvious. Mathew was frail with a slender build; if I squinted my eyes, he had a strong resemblance to Joel Grey from the movie Cabaret. He had a shaved head and always stood with his hands in his front pockets. If he didn't talk, one would barely notice his presence. When he did talk, he was a man of very few words, extremely cautious, which came off as being polite and shy. Bethany, who was very glad to see me, was also reserved, her version of glad, if you didn't know her, was hard to detect. I didn't know if she was arrogant or shy. I eventually found out she was arrogant. But at the time there was so much to take in, I wasn't really able to get a read on anyone. I was just coming out of a traumatic and messy break up. For me to be showing up at all was a huge leap.

Bethany gave me a tour of the mansion. From one empty room to the next. The bones of the house were stunning. I had never been inside an old Hollywood mansion and I was in awe, yet, still wondering why it had no furniture. Bethany saved the backyard for last. And there it was, the answer to the strange mystery—all the furniture, antique lamps, couches, chairs, red leather restaurant booths, books, end tables, mattresses, night stands, clothing, Fiestaware, post war band-aid boxes, kitchen utensils, and just an endless sea of someone's extravagant life—dumped, scattered and abandoned in a Hancock Park backyard. I wondered what the neighbors thought? I could tell that it had been there for years. Rained on, faded and weathered. Bethany could see the stunned look on my face, all these priceless antiques just cast out to rot. She stepped close to me and whispered, "Mathew had a very bad childhood, he hates his parents and doesn't want anything to do with this stuff." It must have been really bad. I couldn't imagine why anyone would throw all these beautiful antiques out like trash. It didn't make sense, and at this point, I didn't want it to, I already knew too much. She also told me not to mention it to Mathew; it was a sensitive subject, "He wishes it would just go away, so he would never have to think about it again." I'd never seen anything like it. But I understood and promised not to say a word.

Their rehearsal was good. Dark, new wave, power pop. Not my thing, I was into local punk bands; the Circle Jerks, X and Fear. Or imports and out-of-towners; The Clash, The Damned, Sex Pistols, Johnny Thunders and The Velvet Underground. I hated new wave, it was an insulting label that I never wanted to be associated with. For what they did, they were great, despite the fact that they had a synthesizer...I just never saw them leaving the living room. Just a gut feeling, that unfortunately for them, turned out to be true.

As I was leaving, Mathew mentioned, if I knew somebody that needed a room to rent, he was looking. It just so happened I was that somebody. My lease was running out and I was looking to move. My boyfriend had just left me for another woman, alone with our guesthouse on San Vicente Avenue, just south of the Sunset Strip, two blocks from the Whisky a Go Go. A great location that I needed to get away from. Despite all it's oddities, finding the pink mansion couldn't have come at a better time, in a matter of days my West Hollywood guesthouse and my failed romance would soon be a memory, left behind so I could move on and start a new life.

I moved into the faded pink mansion at 150 dollars a month, for a charming old Hollywood bedroom, with my own bathroom and a walk-in closet filled with 1950s designer clothes that I found in a random closet just off of the laundry room. Mathew was fine with me keeping and wearing the clothes. This shocked me, because I knew the clothes had belonged to his mother. My bedroom windows overlooked the noir junkyard, which was a little depressing, but the only time it ever really got to me was on gloomy L.A. days. But you get what you pay for.

There were still two empty bedrooms for rent that I would soon get two of my friends to move into—Nick and Jake—both ex-boyfriends. Things were starting to look up. My life was starting to feel better.

Shortly after I moved in, I found out that my ex-boyfriend, Bob, was living a few blocks away with his new girlfriend, Carrie Snodgrass, Neil Young's ex-wife. Knowing this, was torture. What were the odds? The harder I tried to outrun my past, the closer it got. My cat, Crayon, who Bob got in the separation, managed to find me, I guess I was close enough for him to pick-up my scent. It broke my heart. I had to keep taking Crayon back to Bob's house. The fact that he kept finding me had me wondering if he was being neglected? I was so torn, my roommates were allergic to cats, and there was nothing I could do about it. So, I would put Crayon (all five pounds of him) in my Volkswagen, crying the whole way to Bob's house, drop Crayon off, only to have him find his way back to me on a consistent basis.

When Justin came over, he didn't see all the rotting memories of abandoned furniture in the backyard, or a house haunted with Mathew's demons and his mysterious painful past, a house now also haunted with my past, living just down the street. All Justin saw was a cool old Hollywood pink mansion, a good place to party, cool people to party with, and a good place to crash. He immediately made himself at home. Justin's arrival was well received, he was charming and funny, everyone in the house loved him, and as long as he didn't consider his ability to keep us all entertained as part of his rent, all would be well.

Mathew was starting to change, I could tell having a house full of people was making him happy, and there was always a reason to throw a party. So we did, on a nightly basis.

March 5ᵗʰ 1982, seemed like any other normal Friday night. Suburban Lawns and The Brainiacs were playing at the Country Club in Reseda. I wasn't a fan of driving into the Valley, especially to Reseda. Growing up in Pacoima, being from the Valley, I spent my life trying to get out, going back never seemed like a good idea. But my boss and owner of the Zero Zero Club, Wayzata de Camerone, was the Sax player for the Brainiacs. I thought it would be a good idea to show up to support his band and make a little money. So, I put 60 Quaaludes in a Peanuts prescription bottle and told Justin to hold them. He was more than happy to take the job.

When we got to the club, it was already packed and parking was impossible. After driving around for about ten minutes—out of the corner of my eye—I saw a parking spot. Not wanting anyone to grab the space, I impulsively made a left hand turn from the right hand lane. The next thing I know those all too familiar blinding red lights were in my rearview and the sound of a police voice blasting through a megaphone commanding for me to pull over. This was never good. I pulled over right in front of the Country Club. Justin is now panicking. "What do I do with these Quaaludes?" "Put them in the glove box!" Little did I know, he put the bottle to his right on the floor next to his car seat, so when the cop opened his door, the prescription bottle just rolled right out. "Brilliant," I muttered under my breath.

We were done, no getting out of this one. The cop picked up the prescription bottle with *my* name on it, and the next thing I know, we're both being cuffed and stuffed into the back of a police car and on our way to the Van

Nuys Jail. The cops were not very nice, when they put on my handcuffs, they put them on extra tight. Sitting on my hands, I could feel the metal cutting into my back and wrists, my hands got numb from lack of circulation and throbbed in pain. The cops were enjoying this so much that they stopped at 7/11 for some ice cream. They just sat there eating in front of me. Enjoying every bight and talking shop. They were in no hurry. It's as if I wasn't even there. My hands were killing me and I had to pee, and all I could think about was what would happen to us? After an intimate and humiliating body search, some verbal abuse and being treated like a Hazmat risk, they put me in a holding cell with 5 other women and a pay phone. These were working women, and my choice of punk rock attire was not acceptable. There were no Hot Topic stores in the Mall, yet. They couldn't figure me out, to them I looked like a freak—dyed black hair, shoulder length and greased back; black *Trash and Vaudeville* pants tucked into motorcycle boots, with a black t-shirt, Ronald Reagan with a gun on the front, and in blood red letters it spelled out, "Ronald ReaGun, The American Trip." Nothing about me was appealing to them, nothing. I got greeted with, "Well, look at this nightmare." I was getting no love in the Van Nuys jail. They wouldn't even sell me a cigarette.

Not knowing who to call, hoping Justin had gotten resourceful, made bail, and was working on posting my bail. When I checked my status, they told me I'd been bailed out. "That's impossible, I'm still in jail." The nice lady on the phone informed me that a woman named Carrie Snodgrass had just posted my bail, and I would be

35

out by daylight. As I sat there watching the second hand move slowly around the clock face, waiting and waiting as time crawled... another working girl was brought in, and before the jail doors could slam shut she announced, "John Belushi is dead, he OD'd at some Hollywood hotel." I couldn't believe it. I just saw him the other night hanging out with Derf Scratch the bass player of Fear, I just saw him playing drums with the Dead Boys at the Whisky A Go Go, he was everywhere, on a bender and running wild through the Hollywood underground and now he's dead? This was now becoming not your normal Friday night.

The sun was just coming up when Carrie, two very large Biker guys, and Justin bailed me out. Justin was really starting to get on my nerves. I was still pissed at him for not hiding the drugs in a safe place. He did think to call Carrie, which I would never have done. I was the x-girlfriend, and would never think to call her to bail me out of jail. How did Justin know her? Another mystery to add to the pile. To my surprise, Carrie was really sweet. I got the feeling that she felt bad about stealing my boyfriend, and maybe by bailing me out of jail, she just might balance out her Karma.

All I wanted was to go home and get some sleep. Once we were in the car, I noticed Carrie could barely form sentences, it seemed like she could use some sleep herself. It was the first time she and I had ever come face-to-face. I couldn't help but want to study the women who took my man. I felt conflicted, indebted and resentful. Her existence had changed the course of my whole life. I was having a wide range of emotions, and with the lack of sleep and the news that I was being charged with possession with intent to sell (a felony), was trumping everything. My blood pressure was soaring, and yet I could barely keep my eyes open. I felt happy to see her, and also wondered what she had that I didn't? It was now so obvious—my x-boyfriend was a star-fucking punk rocker. Everyone's true colors were starting to show and my belief system was quickly crumbling. Justin couldn't shut up. Freaking out about what would happen to us, or rather, him. All I wanted to do was go home and get some food and sleep, trapped in a car with my savior, my saint, my enemy, two huge bikers that I didn't care to know; and Justin, my rebound, who was looking less and less attractive with every second that passed.

As they were about to drop me off, Carrie asked if she could come in to use my bathroom? Which to me translated to, she wanted to see if there was any traces of Bob in my house, in case he was cheating on her the way he cheated on me. Oh what a tangled web...I had nothing to hide. I actually felt bad for her. I showed her the way to the bathroom, and then gave her a quick tour—trying not to make it seem like a bums rush, but I had been up all night—standing on the spiral staircase she turned to me and suddenly got very lucid. "You know, Bob's still in love with you? Look at you, you're young and beautiful." All I could think was, Not young and beautiful enough, or else why would he leave me? Living with Bob was all I knew, I moved in with him when I was 19, right after my mom came home from Las Vegas on New Year's Day announcing that she'd just got married and was moving out. My Mom ran away from home, so I ran off with Bob to Hollywood. Bob was all the family I knew, I had no net. Without him, I felt lost.

Speechless, I just stood on that staircase, not feeling young or beautiful, just scared and leave-able, facing a felony charge and jail time. I didn't know what to say, except, "Thank you for bailing me out Carrie, I'd still be in there, if it wasn't for you." She gave me motherly hug and left me to get a some sleep. Which was about to be the last time I'd get a good nights sleep for what seemed like an eternity, because every night at 4 a.m. sharp, the visits started. That damn door knocker would pound so lound... and every night like clockwork, I would answer that door and there would be her two big Biker friends.

"Just making sure you haven't skipped town."

They were Carrie's goons. In order to bail us out, Carrie put up the deed to her house, well, if you want to get technical, Carrie put up the deed to Neil Young's house, her x-husband. So I could see why they would want to keep an eye on us. Her house in Hancock Park, unlike the one I lived in, was a beautiful Hancock Park mansion, I was facing a felony, and they were not taking any chances. This went on for about three months. It was starting to become a joke. One time I even greeted them at the door with fresh baked chocolate chip cookies.

"Hi guys, I made you some cookies," I purred.

"Oh great, thanks Iris!!!"

"You're welcome, see you in a few hours."

I wasn't kidding. I'd get a visit from them every four to six hours. They were close by. At one point they sat Justin and I down and made it very clear we would be seeing a lot of them. They interrogated us, asking where we were originally from, all kinds of personal questions about assets and family. I remained calm, but really I was just in shock. I knew I wasn't going anywhere.

It was Justin I was worried about. He was getting squeamish. As time went on his vagina was starting to show. His true colors were coming out, and they were a bright shade of yellow.

As our court date loomed closer, we were both coming undone. Fighting all the time, over small stuff, the weight of a felony hanging over our heads took all the fun out of our fling and the Justin I met that day at the Zero Zero was no longer cute, charming or funny. He was quickly revealing the narcissist, that he truly was. All he cared about was himself and I wanted him gone, but I was stuck with him. The Bikers wouldn't have it any other way, because not only was I indebted to Carrie for bailing me out of jail and needed to show up to that court date, I also had to make sure that Justin showed up as well. This was not fun.

One day, as Justin was throwing one of his daily tantrums, threatening to kill himself. I thought to myself, *this bitch just wants an audience*. As he sat there howling and tearlessly crying. I calmy said, "I'm hungry, I'm going to get a burger. See you later." When I came back fifteen minutes later, poor suicidal Justin was downstairs laughing and joking with my roommates. Busted, I thought! That was it; I was done. Once this court case is over, I never want to see him again. That court date couldn't come fast enough. I wanted this jobless fuck out of my life. It was bad enough I was looking at a felony. His whining was making things even more unpleasant than they already were.

In the meantime, things were starting to deteriorate with Bob and Carrie. Bob was coming by to visit, a lot. Asking to sleep over, hanging around and asking how I was. I got the feeling he was missing the life we once had, the simplicity and the stability. But I couldn't ask. And it was too late. I was already in too deep; the last thing I needed was to throw another wrench into an already twisted situation. We all had our drama, our scars, and our wounds. Bottom line, I was shell-shocked and just trying not to make things worse, trying not to go to jail. In the middle of all the kaos Mathew and I were getting close. He started opening up to me, offering information. As long as I didn't push, he felt safe. Mathew was a kind, and good man. He eventually told me why the furniture was in the backyard; When his parents were in their hey day, they were surrounded by celebrities, they owned a few famous night spots and hosted fabulous soirees at their house on a regular basis. His father was a bad alcoholic and a real bastard to his mom. His mother had been pregnant three times before his birth. Every time, his father was sure that the baby wasn't his and in an alcoholic rage he'd throw Mathew's mother down that beautiful spiral staircase, causing her to miscarry three times in a row. Somehow, Mathew managed to live through the fourth pregnancy, the fourth trip down the staircase. It broke my heart and suddenly I completely understood why he hated that house, hated his parents and hated all those beautiful antiques that lay rotting in the backyard. The story was far more noir than I could ever imagine. It was at this point that I stopped wearing the designer clothes that Mathew let me have, and why all the furniture not only lay to rot in the backyard, but should probably be burned and taken far away from Mathew. Regardless, I also knew that removing all that stuff wasn't going to take away the damage that he'd suffered, or the scars. I also understood why Mathew liked having a full house of people who had nothing to do with his family. We were all there to distract him, all there to give him relief, if only temporary. Mathew was just trying to find himself, and even though he had his musical equipment as a creative outlet, it wasn't enough. He needed more, and after talking with Matherw, I could tell in his quest to find friends and fulfillment, he'd been used a lot along the way. He was too fragile for this world and I don't know if it was his childhood that had made him that way, or he was already that way and his childhood caused him deeper damage.

The Court date finally arrived, we all drove together—Carrie, the two Biker guys, Justin and myself—down to the Van Nuys courthouse. They called Justin's name first, and the judge said, "Charges dropped." I've never seen anyone bolt so fast out of a room. Justin stood up and shouted, "Yes!" And left the room. Not even an obligatory *good luck* to me. I felt numb. Sitting there, as people were talking and shuffling papers. To them, this was just another day, and for me, my life was no longer my own, everything was surreal and in slow motion. As I sat there looking around the room, watching everyone go about their daily lives, I spotted the court reporter. She looked familiar. She was looking at paperwork, it was my paperwork; just then I saw her look up and around the room until she spotted me. Our eyes met and she immediately walked over, "Iris!?, what are you doing here? It's me April Weiss, remember from Branford Park, we grew up together?" I couldn't believe it. I grew up at April's house. She had one of those houses where the parents were never home so the kids took over. Her house was a teen crash pad where we could all drink, smoke pot and have sex. When her parents did come home, they would just step over our passed-out teenage bodies, go to sleep only to wake up to go back to work again the next morning.

April had become a court reporter, and today, she was my court reporter. She asked me the details, and I gave her everything. She told me to stay put and she'd be right back. I watched her walk over to the D.A. They talked back and forth. She pointed me out and then called me over. April introduced us, as we exchanged pleasantries the judge brought down his gavel. I was told to go back to my seat. I could hear my heart beating in my head. They called up one person and then the next. Mouths were moving, but I could hear nothing. Then my name was called, *that* I heard. As I stood before the Judge, he and the D.A. exchanged whispered words, and then the D.A. walked away. The judge looked over my paper work. He then looked up at me. "Iris, you know better than to be driving without a license?"

"Yes sir, I do."

"Iris, do you have a license?"

"Yes Sir, I do."

"May I see it?"

I pulled it out of my wallet. The D.A walked over, grabbed my license and took it to the Judge.

"Nice picture."

"Thank you, your Honor."

He handed my license back to the D.A. "Okay, driving without a license, case dismissed."

"Thank you so much, your Honor."

I couldn't believe it. This was another pivotal snapshot in time that radically changed the course of my life. With weakened knees, I almost collapsed. And as the room was still spinning, I managed to walk back to my seat and sit down. I needed to wait to thank April for being such a lifesaver. We all left, just one big happy family. The drive back from the Valley to Hancock Park was surreal. I couldn't grasp what had just happened. We all couldn't. I felt a huge weight lifted; my life was finally my own again—no more worrying, no more 4 a.m. visits from the two Biker guys, no more babysitting Justin. I could tell Carrie hadn't slept in a while, but she also seemed relieved. I know she must have been stressed the whole time. I could tell she was exhausted. She wasn't making any sense. Whatever words she thought she was saying, were not the words that were coming out of her mouth, infact they weren't words at all.

As they dropped me off, I thanked her and hugged her and told her to get some rest. I hugged the two Biker guys and told them I would miss them. "We can come by tonight at four, if that would make you feel better?" "I'll miss you, but not that much." We all laughed. I got out of the car and waved goodbye as they drove off. I went straight to my bedroom. Justin went with them back to Carrie's house, and that was fine with me. *She can have that one too.*

I was just about to crawl in bed when my phone rang. It was Carrie asking me if I'd seen Bob. I had no clue, and that's what I told her. "Carrie, I'm so sorry, I have no idea, knowing Bob, for all we know he could be hiding in my closet right now." And jokingly I turned my closet door handle to open it, and the door pulled back. I screamed and almost dropped the phone, "Carrie, someone is in my closet, I'm not fucking kidding."

I'm way too tired for this. Please god, why now?

Carrie told me to try again. I grabbed the doorknob with all my strength, and again, it pulled back. The whole time Carrie on the other end of the phone begging to know what was going on! I tried again and this time I won. I got the door open to find Bob, crouched down, stark naked, hiding in my fucking closet. Looking up at me, he could tell I was confused.

"Carrie, Bob's here, do you want to talk to him?"

"Yes!"

I handed the phone to Bob, still crouched down in my closet. Shut the closet door and crawled into bed.

As I started to drift off to sleep, I could hear a mumbling conversation coming from my closet. There was something oddly comforting about it. Just then, I felt my bed shake, it was Crayon, he found me again, curled up next to me, and we both fell asleep...

Driving Miss Crazy
(For Mad Marc Rude, R.I.P.)

"Sometimes things happen in life that are
completely unexplainable, some might even say magical.
This was one of them..."

Hollywood, Ca. July 1990...

I knew taking a cab to buy drugs was a bad idea, but the car was down and we had no other choice. The cab driver wasn't happy about it either. The round trip was probably what tipped him off. When I started to get sick—shivering, shaking, sweating and sneezing—that was the dead give away.

My boyfriend Marc kept saying things like, "She's got a really bad cold man, can we make this fast?" But the driver wasn't having it, and finally he said in his very scolding Persian accent, "I know why she sick, but it no cold, I know what wrong with her!" And then shot me a cold, shaming stare through his rearview mirror. Marc just snarled at him and I continued to shiver and sweat. I wasn't sick when we got in the cab and now it's a game of beat-the-clock. The only thing that kept me going was knowing it would all be over with, in a matter of 30 minutes. On the way back Marc gave me the drugs and I put them in my pack of Marlboros. The ride home was fast and smooth, not too many red lights. The driver dropped us off on our corner and Marc paid him his 20 bucks. He sped off barely waiting for us to close the door. I decided to take that personal.

Still sick but now very excited. Clutching my pack of Marlboros I opened it up to peek inside, and all I could see were cigarettes, the drugs were gone! We ripped the pack to pieces and it just wasn't there. At this point we're both sick and we'd just spent our last money. The only thing we could think was that it had to be in that cab. But the really messed up thing was we couldn't remember the name of the cab company.

So the plan was, for me to drop to my knees and start looking in the street, the gutter and sidewalk in case it fell while I was getting out of the cab. And for Marc to find the nearest payphone and start calling all the cab companies and try to find our cab and see if we could get him to come back. Which was an insane idea. Why would he care? He hated us, but we were sick, desperate and broke, with no other options, what the hell.

So there I was crawling around on all fours doing a thorough pavement search for our lost drugs, right in front of the bar we lived above. It was a popular dive bar called the Shamrock. Located at the east end Hollywood Boulevard, no stars on the sidewalks, no tourist attractions, just us and our drug habits trying to stop time, (not one of my finer moments), living above a bar that was on it's way out, soon to be a strip club. The last thing I wanted was to run into anyone I knew, but, of course, when I really could *not* talk to anybody, an old boyfriend walked out of the bar. I hadn't seen him in six years. The last time I saw him was when I left him for cheating on me, taking all of the furniture, and waking him up to take the bed.

He stood at the end of our driveway wearing only red boxers and a blue Mohawk, yelling half awake, "Where are you going?," In a thick English accent, as I drove off in the U-Haul. *I didn't think he cared?*

He was really happy to see me, which was a pleasant surprise. When he asked me what I was doing, I told him I lost a bracelet that my dead grandmother gave me, and I *had* to find it. The next thing I know he's on all fours helping me, and then to add comedy to this tragedy, two friends of his walked out of the bar, and he gets them to help us look. So now there's four people on their hands and knees crawling around in the street and the gutter and three of them are looking for a lost family heirloom that doesn't exist. Marc's having trouble finding the cab company and these three guys crawling around with me are starting to get on my nerves. As guilty as I felt, I couldn't tell them what I was really looking for because they might find it and keep it. And we couldn't have that...

After about twenty minutes of searching, which felt like an eternity, out of nowhere, our cab, the one we think we possibly lost our drugs in, came flying around the corner at top speed. The only reason he stopped was to keep from running us all over. I was so happy to see that asshole. Even though he didn't believe the lost family heirloom story and hated our guts on general principal, he still let us rip out the back seat of his cab. Which was bizarre in itself. And after a quick minute, there it was, the drugs!

Sometimes things happen in life that are completely unexplainable, some might even say magical. This was one of them...Did we deserve it?, absolutely not! Did we need it?, most definitely!"

Dumb fucking junkie luck, is what I thought, and definitely somewhat of a religious experience, Marc and I both agreed that it was proof of God or maybe even the devil, and whichever one it was, he, she or it definitely wanted us to get high and get well!

And so we did, just in time for twilight—my favorite time of day—and as the sun went down and the lights of Hollywood slowly flickered on, sparkling a little extra that night. We looked out over the city with a perfect view of the Hollywood Sign, and laughed at our good fortune, once again all was right with a world that was wrong. And as we slipped into a velvet nod, with the smell of sulfur, cigarette smoke and Night-Blooming Jasmine in the air...we danced in the trenches.

It was only a matter of time.

Brandford Park

Navigating my family as a child always felt like some kind of emotional video game, like driving on a freeway where everyone's speeding and changing lanes without using their blinkers. It was exciting and exhausting. By the time I was six I needed a cigarette and a cocktail, but of course that didn't happen; I had to wait till I was eleven, like all the other kids on the block.

We grew up in Pacoima, California, in the San Fernando Valley, the S.F.V. Known for being a locus of poverty and crime, and put on the map by singer, songwriter, Ritchie Valens, known for is hit song La Bamba. Valens died in a plane crash in 1959 at the age of 17 along with fellow musicians, Buddy Holly and The Big Bopper. The plane crash went down in history as *The Day The Music Died*. To this day Valens is known as the pride of Pacoima, and probably one of only good things that ever came out of that place.

I grew up with three older brothers, and the only girl. Which was both a blessing and a curse. They were all in gangs and car clubs. Most of the time I was protected by their reputations, most of the time.

When I was a kid, it felt like I had three extra fathers, but no one—not even my father—was officially assigned the position. Throw in the massive age differences, a 13 year stretch between my oldest brother and myself, the literal gaps in generations had them understand me a lot less and worry about me a lot more. When I was still on training wheels, and learning to tie my shoes, they (of course) didn't want me around. Their lives were far too much for my toddler eyes and ears. They were doing and saying things that couldn't be heard or repeated. They hung out together, dressed alike and immaculate. 501s starched, pressed and cuffed, Pendleton's, and wingtips, shined meticulously, spotless. Presenting a united front and a force to be reckoned with, looking like they stepped out of the pages of Low Rider Magazine.

A lot of the neighborhood girls had crushes on them. Befriending me, in futile attempts to meet my brothers and their friends. Guys either feared or respected them. It's amazing I ever lost my virginity. I didn't know it at the time, but I was living in my own private monastery. Guys were actually afraid to approach me. Don, the youngest of the three, was in a gang called the Branford Park Boys, named after the park just around the block—a cigarette walk from our front doorstep and our second home. Branford Park was known for being a dangerous free-for-all. The place where I had my first drink and blackout at the age of 10, first smoked pot at the age of 11, first dropped acid at the age of 12, and smoked my first cigarette somewhere in between.

It was also the place where I almost got raped and beat up pretty bad at the age of 10. It was broad daylight when five guys dragged me into a dark rec room. They were just about to rip my clothes off when the park's director Mr. Ortiz heard my screams. I never told anyone, but mysteriously, one of their homes burnt down to the ground the following week.

Basically, the park was the place where we could always find any drug and others like us, whose parents weren't around to notice we were all growing up way too fast down at Branford Park. And Don's gang was named after it.

Paul, the middle brother, was in a car club called The Pagans, and Marty, the oldest brother, was in The Satan "something or others", the name escapes me right now. Our house, which was basically a Chop Shop with a Pool Table, was the neighborhood hangout. Always packed with all the neighborhood tough guys, telling war stories while drinking beer, cheating each other at poker and endless games of pool, in a smoke cloud haze of Marlboros and marijuana. There were always about four cars in the driveway, one up on blocks on the front lawn, and two parked curbside. '63 Thunderbirds and '64 Impalas waiting to get painted, tinted, chopped, and lowered. And a couple of motorcycles scattered in parts. I can still hear the comforting sounds of the break of the pool balls, and the clinking of beer bottles as Motown music played in the background.

One time my mom came to pick me up from Junior high School in Don's lowered, yellow & white '54 Chevy Bellaire. Windows tinted and in mint condition, because her car was in the shop. I was so embarrassed. I got in and slid all down to the floor on the shotgun side, praying that none of my friends would see me. The best part was watching her slow way down for bumps and dips, because that car was so damn low to the ground. It had glass packs, so the engine was loud, like a big wet purr. To this day that sound still gives me a warm fuzzy. I have to admit she looked pretty hot driving that car. She was young, beautiful and bottle blonde with her hair piled high to the sky. She divorced my dad when I was three, had he been around, the atmosphere would have been drastically different. A tight ship, there would be no clubhouse, and definitely no chop shop.

I followed my mother everywhere, wanting to be just like her. Glued to her every move. I used to love watching her get ready to go out on dates, mesmerized, by her transformation as she performed her magic. The many times I watched her leave the house in a cloud of Chanel No. 5, into the Hollywood night. My imagination ran wild, envisioning klieg lights, red carpets and cocktail parties with movie stars and starlets. All the men looked like Frank Sinatra and Dean Martin. And all the women wore gloves looking like Jackie O or Marilyn Monroe. And my mother was one of them, with some man that might someday be my new father. They were all so creepy and never good enough.

One of them named Steve would always bring me a Dixie cup filled with change, asking for a kiss in return. After a month went by, during our polite ritual, he slipped me the tongue. I backed up like a wet cat. Even though I never mentioned it, we never saw Steve again.

There was no shortage of men to take his place, as my mother spent her Saturday nights looking for Mr. Good Enough. Leaving me at the mercy of my brothers, and many times, they'd leave me at the mercy of their friends. But I loved it. They weren't as protective as my brothers, allowing me to hear and see things that were normally off limits, and I had crushes on them all, while they just treated me like a punk kid, until I blossomed and filled out my halter top—it was night and day. Suddenly, they were treating me different. After all those years of being teased or invisible, I finally got the attention I longed for, and I didn't want it anymore. Life is funny that way.

We *were* the bad house on the block. Broken cars and broken dreams, with always some kind of commotion going on, always in some state of emergency. If the police weren't showing up all hours of the night—looking for my dad, one of my brothers and eventually me—it was a subpoena server, an ambulance, or the fire department! One day in particular, my mom and I came home from the Broadway in a cab, our house was on fire, due to some experimenting my brothers were doing in the garage. According to my mom, she told the cab driver to just keep driving.

Along with of all this crazy activity, It was a common occurrence (like clockwork), an angry neighborhood mother would come pounding on our door to inform our mother, "Control your kids and keep them away from my children, next time I'm calling the cops!" This happened at least once a week. Scarring the other kids and playing practical jokes was a family pastime, but always at the expense of some poor kid, who was smaller and defenseless. Always taking the bait. Like the time they made little Buddy Anderson stand in a puddle of water and put two live wires together, electrocuting him. Nothing serious, but his mother was not happy, and we never saw buddy again.

Or the time we got kicked out of Busch Gardens during the tour. There we were—on the catwalk above the massive vats of boiling beer—as the tour guide was explaining the brewing process, out of the corner of my eye, I saw my brother Paul elbow my brother Don, mouthing the words,

"Watch this."

As quietly as he could, he gathered up all the saliva from the back of his throat, hawking the biggest loogie over the rail into one of the massive bubbling beer vats. The next thing I know, the whole family is being escorted out of Busch Gardens, in front of all the other families, as security walked my brothers out by the backs of their collars and my mother smacking them all the way to the car. The people got their money back, ruining the tour for everyone. It must have cost Busch Gardens thousands to replace the contaminated beer, if they bothered. My mother was so mad she made my brothers walk home. This happened on a regular basis, we couldn't go anywhere without breaking something, escalators, elevators, nothing was safe. We were bad, but this was the price that came with being part of an unruly family. Teaching me at an early age not to show my feelings, like I just didn't care.

This was my family. The same brothers that knocked me around, were the same brothers that protected me. Conflicted from all sides because, despite all the crazy and tough times, whether we liked each other or not, no matter what—we stuck together.

I don't talk about it with my brothers much. We buried a lot of it when we buried my Dad. Sometimes I think they don't even remember. Once in a while, I'll bring something up, and they'll just give me a glazed over look and say, "God Iris, how do you remember?" And I'll think, God, how could you forget?

It's all so hard to believe, my nice normal family. It feels like another lifetime and another family. Amazingly enough, they all came out unscathed and, well, I kind of didn't. I internalized a lot of it and feel a little stuck still trying to piece it all together, still looking for that heart-shaped watch on a chain my dad gave me, that I lost, with a lot of other valuable things, not so material, down at Branford Park.

Hollywood in The 1980s

Hollywood in the eighties was the constant ringing of the telephone, asking to get on the guest list. Or it was a busy signal with no call waiting. There were no cell phones and barely any answering machines. By the mid-eighties the beeper showed up, but there were definitely no computers. Everything we did was DIY.

For writers, if we needed to do research, it meant driving to the library. Band flyers, fanzines, and chapbooks were all done at Kinko's, where we setup a trade with the Kinko's workers, free printing for free drinks at the bars we worked at, and they were on the guest list for life at any clubs our bands played. Then we'd take our bartered chapbooks and sell them for drinks at the bars.

Since there was no Internet and no cell phones, when we wanted to connect with people, we went places. Places like The Masque, or Blackie's, the Anti-Club, Club 88, the Brave Dog, where I met Andy Warhol, the Atomic Café next door, and Al's Bar just down the street. There was the Vex—come for the show stay for the riot—and Oki Dog, which always felt like an eighties version of Arnolds from Happy Days, but instead of fifties Greasers, it was punk rock, chicken hawks and the passing parade of rough trade, where everyone went after the Starwood, which was a great place to see a variety punk bands, metal and new wave bands. Owned by the notorious Eddie Nash, and closed down due to the "Hammer Murders" in Laurel Canyon.

There was the Cathay de Grande, where I had my first bartending job. My roommate Pleasant told the owner that I had tons of experience. I knew how to make a Screwdriver and just faked the rest. It was the Cathay. People either drank beer or whiskey shots. Or whatever they could sneak in. I remember my first night. Top Jimmy and Jeffrey Lee Pierce were spinning records. They would go back and forth—play some crazy country song and then they'd play some horrible metal song—for hours, at unbearably loud volumes. It was killing my ears and every time someone would try to order a drink, I'd have to yell back at the top of my lungs, "WHAT DID YOU SAY?" And then do my best to read their lips. I kept asking and eventually begging Jeffrey Lee and Top Jimmy to lower the music. Every time I'd ask, they'd just make it louder and laugh in my face, like 10 year old boys. I was yelling so much, that my throat started to hurt and I could barely speak. Finally I got so mad that I walked over to Jeffrey Lee and Top Jimmy with a full pitcher of beer, and politely, through gritted teeth I asked them, one more time, to please lower the music? They both looked at me, and mouthed the words, "WHAT DID YOU SAY, WE CAN'T HEAR YOU, THE MUSIC IS KINDA LOUD?" Laughing maniacally, turning it up louder. So I took the pitcher of beer and slowly poured it over both turntables. It lowered the music all right; it stopped it altogether. Smoke came out of the mixing board. They sat there stunned.

"I told you guys to lower the fucking music!" I turned around and huffed off! Somehow, I didn't get fired.

But, it was pretty hard to get fired from the Cathay de Grande. There was Raji's, our Honeycomb Hideout, thanks to Dobbs the owner and former doorman and bartender at the Cathay de Grande. Dobbs treated everyone like family, so it felt more like a clubhouse than a nightclub. The real action at Raji's happened either in the back alley, Dobbs' office or in the kitchen when The The Vandal's original singer Stevo was manning the grill.

There was Len Fagan's Coconut Teaser, where Len treated everyone that played there like royalty. Baba's famous "Jam Night" every Sunday at the Soundcheck on the corner of Sunset and Vine. Always a wild time, but so were the other six nights of the week. Having a mix of older bar regulars, bookies, drug dealers, musicians and scenesters made for an interesting combination. Baba made everyone feel right at home. The Soundcheck only had two rules; no hats and no wearing colors, which was code for; no pimps, no bikers and no gangs.

The Soundcheck was also an Eddie Nash club, along with the Music Machine and the Seven Seas on Hollywood Boulevard, not the coolest place to hang out, just a big dance club. Where Ricky Rachtman—MTV's heavy metal host for Headbangers Ball—got his start as a DJ. There was the Club Lingerie where Brendan Mullen—the founder of The Masque—booked a wide variety of music, everything from Big Joe Turner, Screamin' Jay Hawkins and Percy Mayfield to Junkyard, Thelonious Monster, The Little Kings, and everything in between. I usually entered that place through the backdoor. If I wasn't interested in the band, I was either drinking out back in the alley with friends, or I was backstage because on many nights, that's where the real party was. The Lingerie by far, had one of the best backstage areas in town.

There was the Scream Club. The first one

downtown at the Embassy Hotel, where we never knew if we were in the ladies' room or the men's room, because both seemed coed. The second Scream was across the street from MacArthur Park, and the third was at the Probe in Hollywood, also home of Ricki Rachtmans' Cat House.

There was and still is; The Whisky a Go Go and The Roxy on the Sunset Strip, next door to the Rainbow Bar & Grill, best known for its incredible pizza and the 2 a.m. parking lot scene, to find all the afterhours parties and once upon a time, a good place to buy Quaaludes. Barney's Beanery in West Hollywood, the well-known historic Tinsel Town eatery was a great place to soak up old ghosts and local punk rock color. It was definitely at the end of a long Hollywood historic run that had seen many decades of celebrity anecdotes and 86'd it's fair share of rock stars. Opening its doors in 1927 on Route 66, before it became Santa Monica Boulevard. Catering to old Hollywood celebrities, artists and writers. By the 1960s the clientele changed with the landscape. Bar stools that were once inhabited by Rita Hayworth, Judy Garland and Errol Flynn were replaced by Jim Morrison, Janice Joplin and Charles Bukowski. Legend has it that Jim Morrison was thrown out for urinating on the bar and Janis Joplin had her last drink there the night she died.

The Beanery's most controversial legacy was its matchbooks that plainly read, "No Faggots Allowed." Before it was officially Boys' Town and before the term Politically Incorrect was in existence. Although Barney's is still there, their matchbooks are not!

Just west of the Beanery was Flippers Roller Rink where bands played in the center of the rink. I remember seeing the bands 999 and Madness play there, and just down the street was the Tropicana Motel with Dukes Coffee Shop underneath. Where Tom Waits and Chuck E. Weiss were permanent residents in the seventies, and where all the touring bands stayed, many times longer then they expected. At any hour of the day or night there was always something going on at the Tropicana. with its black swimming pool and their lenient management that favored the rock 'n' roll clientele. And for the hungry, diehard nighthawks, Canter's Deli (also still there) and Ben Franks, both open 24 hours.

The Zero Zero Club on Cahuenga and its four offshoots were incredible. Even though they were only open on Friday and Saturday night, it meant that just because everything else closed at 2 a.m., the night still didn't have to end. They were all illegal afterhours speakeasies, all opened at 2 am, and all stayed open till sun up, a police raid, or whenever the beer ran out, whichever came first.

I tended bar at a few of them. The one on Vine and the one on Hollywood Boulevard were part owned by David Lee Roth of Van Halen. Whenever there was a police raid, being the bartender, I was a target for the police and usually one of the first to be tipped off by the doorman—whether it was Marc Rude, Big Jason or Carlos Guitarlos—who would come straight to the bar, unscrew the overhead light bulb, and before they could say, "Honey the cops are here, run!," I was already pouring the contents of my tip jar into my purse to get the fuck out. The police raids there were hilarious; it was hard to keep a straight face. As the cops had everyone in a lineup, from the likes of David Lee Roth, Top Jimmy, Althea Flynt, Bill Gazzarri, Taquila Mockingbird, Vandal's original singer Stevo, photographer Gary Leonard, and members of the Red Hot Chili Peppers, Social Distortion, X, The Blasters, T.S.O.L., Fear, Guns N' Roses, L.A. Guns, The Hangmen, The Ringling Sisters, Junkyard, Tex & The Horseheads, The Screamin' Sirens, The Hickoids, The Lame Flames, The Little Kings, Fishbone, and every punk rocker and metal head from Hollywood to Huntington Beach. With hands over heads waiting to be frisked, as pills, bindles of drugs, vials of coke and syringes came flying out of nowhere, hitting the ground at a breakneck speed. Luckily we had a good friend who was a bail bondsmen, so no one stayed locked up too long.

There was the Frolic Room and its spinoffs. The original Frolic next to the Pantages Theatre at Hollywood and Vine and Bob's Frolic #2 on Wilcox and Hollywood Boulevard across the street from Playmates Of Hollywood lingerie store with the third Zero One Club right above it. There was the Vine Bar & Grill next to The Brown Derby with all the Hirschfeld's of the stars covering the walls. And a few doors down was the Firefly that had a doorman checking IDs. If it was your birthday the doorman would alert the bartender from his walkie-talkie and the bartender would set the bar on fire and everyone in the whole place would sing you "Happy Birthday." It was a long-standing tradition, living up to its name, the Firefly. Then, of course, there were the crash pads; the Canterbury, the Oxford House, and the Garden Court Apartments on Hollywood Boulevard, where after decades of decline and completely abandoned, in the early eighties it became a squat for punk rock runaways and gang bangers, it was known on the streets as Hotel Hell. In its heyday the Garden Court Apartments represented the Golden Age of Hollywood, opening its doors on New Years Eve, 1919, to residents; Stan Laurel and Oliver Hardy, John Barrymore, Louis B. Mayer and Lillian Gish, to name a few.

Then there was where I lived—Disgraceland—with band member and writing partner Pleasant Gehman, Tex & The Horseheads' guitartist Mike Martt and Screamin' Sirens bassist Laura Bennett, and a revolving door of many other roommates. The scene of so many crazy

64

nights that lasted for days, and like all notorious punk rock crash pads, Disgraceland was where bands from out of town would come and stay way longer than they planned. Where Don Bolles, drummer for the Germs, lived in our driveway in his white van with his personalized license plates that read "UNIT666." He ran extension cords through my bedroom window to power his alarm clock so he could wake up on time for his job at the L.A. Weekly. Disgraceland was also the place where everyone came after all the clubs closed. Around 2:30 a.m. like clockwork there would be that inevitable knock at the front door, always, about 30 people standing drunk on the porch, waiting to pile in, not wanting the night to end.

Red's Baroque Books—just off Hollywood Boulevard on Las Palmas—was truly a goldmine. Red was known for his incredible Bukowski collection, years before Barfly and before anyone knew who Bukowski was. His shelves were also lined with all the beat and expatriate classics with hard covers that were signed. Red only let you in his store if he liked you. And if he didn't like you he wouldn't let you in. Red's bookstore was truly an important place. He was the last holdout from another time. His bookstore was integral. He gave me and my friends who barely finished high school, a place to learn about real literature and it's lineage. He was always giving us books, making sure we had the knowledge and the literary guidance that we didn't and wouldn't get in school. Red shot straight from the hip and didn't mince his words. He could see that we were hungry for literature. He really cared. Red's Baroque Books was one of those places that changed my life and one of the most important stops along the way in Hollywood during the eighties.

Janet Cunningham's C.A.S.H. Club—home for wayward punkers who didn't have parents or their parents couldn't deal or just didn't care—was another important stop along the way. Janet generously opened up her home, giving so many not only a place to stay, but also a way to make money. The first one opened on Cahuenga Boulevard, a few doors down from the first Zero Zero Club. The second one was on Hollywood Boulevard. Janet was smart. She started a casting agency, for casting agents that needed punkers for movie extras, but were too afraid to round us all up. The movies were mostly big club scenes, which meant we were doing what came natural; hanging out, drinking, smoking, playing cards and practical jokes, but getting paid for it! We would get our paychecks and just laugh. And then we'd go home and wash off the residue that covered our bodies from the constant use of the smoke machines, that Hollywood used to create a "nightclub" atmosphere. Because once upon time you could smoke in nightclubs. I'm pretty sure the chemicals used to recreate that smoky atmosphere was probably far more toxic than actual secondhand smoke.

There was the Loyal Order of the Water Buffalo. A men's club for the punk rock music scene, started by Chris Bailey, drummer for The Little Kings, and members of Tex & The Horseheads; Mike Martt, Smog Vomit and Rock Vodka. Basically what qualified you for membership as a Water Buffalo, you had to pass the scrotum drill, ruling out all women. The Water Buffaloes were a punk rock tribute to the Flintstones, with Chris Bailey as the Grand Poobah. They held beauty pageants and BBQs with three-legged races and pie eating contests, wearing loincloths and other jungle attire. Usually held at Griffith Park or Elysian Park—fistfights and blackouts, always guaranteed.

Anything that was worth doing, happened after midnight. It was a time when the headlining acts went on last and there was no pay to play. The record industry was upside down, not knowing what to do next with this "punk rock" music. They could wrap their heads around new wave and metal, but punk rock was too violent.

What I remember best about the eighties was an abandoned Hollywood Boulevard where my friends and I could run amuck and people crossed the streets because they saw us coming.

In the mid eighties punk rock got sideswiped by metal and the two merged, which meant that everyone got their hands on a can of Aqua Net hairspray and teased the shit out their hair and fucked a little more with the ozone.

For me, the eighties was a simple time, red lipstick, blue-black hair dye and black fishnets, that's all I needed. Oh, and some heroin to keep the feelings down. The whole reason I ran off to punk rock was because I had nowhere else to go, 18 years old and on my own. My mom remarried and ran away from home. So I ran off to punk rock, (not with a rebel heart but with a broken heart), and heroin to keep the feelings down.

As the eighties came to and end, things changed. Thurston Moore from Sonic Youth brought Geffen Records a Nirvana record, and that's when Grunge was born. Much to the dismay of the metal scene. I say this was the end of the eighties, but let's be honest the eighties didn't really end until 1992.

And now it's 2012, a whole new century, and here I sit writing this on my lap top computer with my iPhone next to me, my hair a nice shade of blonde, plugged into the internet, and no heroin in sight.

But I can still remember Movies Til Dawn on Channel 5, The Three Stooges were always on Channel 13 and there was *only* 6 channels to choose from. TV usually ended around 2 a.m. First you'd see the Indian with "America The Beautiful" playing in the background and then, there would be nothing but white snow, and a loud static sound. That was the worst. We'd race to the TV to turn it off before the snow came, because it was scary...as if the whole world had come to an end. But not to worry, bright an early at 6 a.m., it would start all over again, with some nice normal news program or Romper Room, and then if we were lucky, we would go to sleep...

Daddy's Girl

He despised humanity
or the lack of
had no patience for it
whatsoever
except when it came to
homeless men and women
and people living on skid row
He could be someone's worst enemy

or their greatest friend.

He was
my first love
and my first heartbreak.
my biggest fan
and I his.
He was
my greatest teacher
and the perfect tour guide.
I remember our trips
when I was five
Just the two of us

from the Pacific Ocean

down the Sunset Strip

pointing out all the

Hollywood Glamour spots

Like Dino's

and The Playboy Club.

All the way

to Downtown L.A.

as he would announce,

"Last stop, Skid Row."

and he'd give me quarters

to pass out

to the homeless,

telling me, "Iris, this is it, this is real life.

Those who can afford it, don't understand it.

And those who understand it, can't afford it."

He was a real Robinhood.

A hustler with a heart of gold

giving the shirt off his back

and the heart on his sleeve.

But, he loved to get over

thrived on it

even down to the little things

like long lines at the movies

he would use his wounded vet story
and it got us in every time…

Most of our food, furniture and appliances were gotten off, "the back of a truck." I remember when we got our first color TV/stereo console, my mother screaming, "Don't get used to it because it's probably hot!"

Then there were the more humorous times, when he got us a brand new living room set. The fact that he was colorblind made for an interesting selection. We had a bright orange reclining chair, clashing with a loud floral print couch and a plaid loveseat, and we lived with it—that's the funny part.

Or the time he went to a car lot for a "test drive" because his car was in the shop, and he needed to get my brother Marty to the high school dance. As he drove off the car lot he shouted the words, "Don't worry, I'm a home owner." Only to return the car three days later.

He was extremely excessive, I once asked him for a piece of gum and he brought back from the store six cases of Bazooka Joe, 6,000 in a case, that's 36 thousand pieces of bubble gum. It's amazing I still have teeth.

After they divorced, my mother never let him in the house. He never quite got over it, but he still came around; I just had to talk to him on the driveway. I thought this was normal until I saw an episode of Father Knows Best.

He was never one to remember my birthday, but he'd always show up a few months later with some grandiose gift like 200 silver dollars and a brand new Schwinn bicycle. Trying to make up for lost time.

I didn't see too much of him in my teens. He left town.. When I was 26 he died in a car crash. He was on his way to pick me up for dinner. I hadn't seen him in a long time. When they pulled him from the wreck, the car exploded and the only form of identification was my address and phone number in his pocket. When the hospital called with a description of their John Doe, I knew right away it was him.

He was a complex man with a Damon Runyonesque, P.T. Barnum kind of charm. He had a goodness deep down inside of him, never showing any pain, always the super hero, with a rage of steel. He was a proud, proud man. When I saw him laying on that hospital bed, held together by tubes. I thought, this isn't how it's supposed to be. I thought for sure he would wake up. But this was it. This is how the story ends.

I never expected him to leave this earth so early on in life. I wouldn't be the person I am if it weren't for him. He was a man of the streets and his words and wisdom have not gone forgotten. He had the uncanny ability to sum up people in a matter of seconds. He was a complicated man with simple needs. He never stopped loving my mother and to this day, no one has ever loved me like he did and I don't think anyone ever will. He was a hard act to follow, making it hard for all the rest.

Before they lowered his coffin into the ground, I placed 12 Iris' in there with him. I know he would have liked that. And as the years go by, the loss of him never gets easier, I only miss him more.

Life at Disgraceland... "Iris, I Need You!"

Growing up with 3 older brothers definitely had its advantages. No one ever messed with me. I learned how to play poker at the age of eight, shuffle a mean deck of cards, and whistle really loud with two fingers, all by age 10. It also had its disadvantages, because—they tortured the hell out of me, and they were good at it.

Don collected skulls of all shapes and sizes. One skull in particular was the size of a bowling ball and glowed in the dark. We shared a bedroom and that skull was scary. No way could I sleep with that thing glowing and threatening my existence. I begged my Mom to make him put it away, which worked for about five minutes. As soon as she left the room, out came the skull.

Of all my brothers, Don was the biggest torture king of them all. Unfortunately for me, Don was the one always elected to babysit. On really cold, gloomy days—when he and I were home alone—he had a routine...down our very long, creepy hallway, lined with clown paintings hanging every inch of the way, (the kind with the eyes that followed you). Don would go all the way down to the far end of the hallway and eerily, over and over, like a ghost, call my name, "Iiiirrriiisssss, oh Iiiiirrrriiisssss." I was eight years old and fell for it every time. Blindly and innocently, I would go down that hallway. Don would grab me, throw me into my mom's bedroom, turn off the lights, and slam the door shut. It was so dark! Panic would set in, but I would eventually find the light switch, open the door, and dart out of the house.

I sat on our front curb for hours in the cold, waiting for my mom to get home, because I was not going back inside that house with that madman. This kind of brotherly torture continued until the day I moved out.

In the summer of 1984 when I moved into Disgraceland. It's hard to say who exactly lived there. A lot of revolving roommates and bands in and out of the place. The décor was like most crash pads... a lot of mattresses everywhere, posters slapped on walls upside down, records (out of their sleeves, laying all over the floor), empty beer cans and bottles rolling around, curtains hanging crooked, curtains that used to be white, now a dingy grayish/beige. One wall had a large display of maxi-pad Tampax spelling out Mr. T., smeared with some kind of red substance resembling blood. There was a bust of Elvis on the mantle with an Alice Cooper makeover and a Christmas tree still up six months after the fact. The tree was decorated with bras, garter belts, old cigarette butts, and at one time, my diaphragm on top in place of a star. I wondered where that went.

Yes, this was where I lived. Walking through Disgraceland was like playing a game of leapfrog over unknown bodies and last night's debris. It was a crazy place...

My room was in the back at the end of a really long, dark red hallway, much like the scary hallway I grew up with. Some of my roommates were Pleasant Gehman, Mike Martt, Laura Bennett, Clam Lynch, Bob Forrest, Stevo Jensen, may he rest in peace, and all of Poison 13, who were visiting from Austin for a week and ended up staying for a month.

They all picked up on my deep-rooted childhood fears, they could smell it like dogs. For fun, they liked to do things like chase me through the house with large, sharp kitchen knives as the theme from Psycho blasted at full volume. I would always manage to escape into my room—close the door and lock myself in—as the knives were still hacking their way in through the cracks of my door.

Clam once told me there was a family of evil clowns living under my bed. To prove it, he demonstrated by putting a plate full of chocolates under the bed to feed them. Minutes later, he pulled out the plate showing me that the chocolates had little bites taken out of them.

"They like chocolate,"

Clam said, in a soft an evil tone .a one particularly awful day, I had a date coming to pick me up—it was our first date. He'd never been to my house. When he arrived, Clam, Laura, Pleasant, Mike Martt and Chris Gates (whose best described as looking like an ax murderer) were all standing over me with large kitchen knives in their hands, banana slices in their eyes... and, of course, the theme to Psycho, blasting throughout the house. They chased me down. Mike, Clam & Chris, had me pinned to my bed, waving knives in my face, while Pleasant and Laura were giving me hickeys on my neck and screaming at the top of their lungs, "Iris, I need you!" it was like Clockwork Orange and Night of the Living Dead. My date was speechless. And maybe a little turned on.

Things only got worse. It got so bad, in order to get a good nights sleep, I resorted to putting two padlocks on my bedroom door from the inside.

I resorted to finding little quiet ways of revenge. I left exploding cigarettes scattered throughout the house. It was great, I'd be lounging and reading in my room, free from any blame, when out of nowhere I'd hear a little explosion and screams of shock. I loved it!

Things eventually quieted down. It seemed like everyone had had enough and maybe they were going to stop torturing me, or maybe they were just playing possum; I couldn't be sure, only time would tell.

After a few months, it was still pretty quiet. I woke up on a warm summer afternoon. As the church bells were ringing, I could hear children playing from the school across the street. I stretched long and slow—this was the first good night's sleep I'd had in a long time. There was a warm wind coming through my window as I lay there peacefully deciding whether to get up or sleep a little longer. Ah, what the hell, I thought, I'll get up. It was such a beautiful day.

When I opened my eyes, there it was... the worst thing they had ever done. Laying next to me, staring me dead in the face, was a wide-eyed Jerry Mahoney ventriloquist dummy with a noose around his neck and a note on his chest secured with a switchblade. And in large red menacing letters—the note read,

"IRIS, I NEED YOU!"

As I lay there screaming and trying to catch my breath,

my life started to pass before me... all my childhood trauma, glowing skulls, evil-eyed clowns chasing me through endless, dark hallways. All of it swirling around in my head like a bad Fellini nightmare. In a moment of sharp clarity, I thought to myself,

Fuck this!

And just then—at that very second—out of the corner of my eye I swear I saw that creepy dummy wink at me.

It was probably just the wind? Right?

Just to be on the safe side, I took the switchblade and stabbed that dummy a few more times

and began plotting my revenge...

The Beat Motel

We were packing our bags with an hour left before checkout time. Leaving the Beat Motel was always hard. We rang in the New Year at a friend's annual bash in Joshua Tree just eleven hours prior. 2006 was officially over.

The Beat Motel in Desert Hot Springs, California had become my getaway, the perfect place to shut out the world, get some writing done, and get a good dose of Beat history. An incredible bed and breakfast, with a theme and ambiance that couldn't, and still can't be found anywhere else.

The Beat Motel was a tribute to the Beat Hotel in Paris that opened its doors in 1933. A small, forty-two room, dark and rundown, "class 13" no star hotel, which meant the owners only met the minimum health and safety codes required by law.

For a surcharge, one could get hot water on Thursdays, Fridays, and Saturdays, if they wanted a hot bath. There was only one bathtub on the premises situated on the ground floor. Meaning if a guest wanted a bath they needed to make a reservation in advance.

The linens were allegedly changed once a month, rats ran freely through the halls, and it was always a good idea when walking the halls to look down, because people were known to slip and fall on dog shit.

In the 1950s, the United States was being subjected to the McCarthy era and the Hollywood Blacklist. The atmosphere in the States was repressive, and the aggressive need of censorship didn't leave much room for artistic freedom. The beauty of being in Paris and living at the Beat Hotel was the freedom it offered to young American writers and artists. Allowing more possibility of expression. If you were an artist of any kind, this made

Paris an exciting place to be.

The hotel was mainly inhabited by; expatriate artists, writers, musicians, pimps and prostitutes. The tenants could paint and decorate their rooms however they wanted and often paid their rent with works of art or literary manuscripts.

Allen Ginsberg and Peter Orlovsky fled to the Beat Hotel in 1957 after exiling themselves during the censorship trial of Ginsberg's book Howl and Other Poems. Ginsberg wasn't on trial; "Howl" was, which meant Ferlinghetti was on trial for publishing the controversial book through his publishing company, City Lights Books. Shortly after Ginsberg and Orlovsky"'s arrival, other beat writers followed. William Burroughs, Gregory Corso, and Harold Norse, along with so many others.

The hotel didn't have a name at this point. It was simply referred to by its address, 9 Rue Gît-le-Cœur. The Beat Hotel was a nickname given by Gregory Corso, and it stuck. It's where Ginsberg wrote parts of "Kaddish", Corso wrote the mushroom cloud-shaped poem, "Bomb" and where Burroughs completed "Naked Lunch", putting the Beat Hotel on the map.

With the triumph of Ferlinghetti in the *Howl* censorship trial, on October 3, 1957 artistic freedom in the United States was restored. The Beat Hotel closed its bohemian doors in 1963.

* * *

The Beat Motel in Desert Hot Springs was more than just a bed and breakfast with an honorable name. The owner

Steve Lowe, in his youth, assisted Burroughs at the peak of his career. Steve had acquired many pieces of Burroughs' "shotgun art" and signed hardcover copies of all the beat classic books, keeping them in glass cases.

Lowe collected writings, artworks, photographs, and memorabilia for his museum-style reception room. Original paintings, glass cases with gunshot spray-paint cans, and a Burroughs adding machine invented by Burroughs' grandfather. Steve Lowe could have kept his collectibles to himself, but he was far too generous, enthusiastic, and respectable. He wanted to make it all available for others to appreciate, allowing the legacies of these great artists and writers to live on. Every time I went to the Beat Motel, Steve and I would sit for hours talking about Beat history. I'd never met anyone more fascinating.

Each room at the Beat Motel was decorated with 1950s furniture. Not just any second-hand, restored collectables, each piece had a story. An ordinary 1950s desk was not ordinary at all; it was the desk that William Burroughs wrote Naked Lunch on. Every room had at least one old typewriter in it that at one time had been used by Ginsberg, Kerouac, Corso, or Burroughs.

The Desert Hot Springs motel was quite different from its dingy, rat-infested namesake. Even the building itself was an architectural gem. The architect who built the precious getaway was John Lautner, known for his Googie architecture, his atomic age style, diners, gas stations, and car washes. Lautner was never given his due credit. Only after his death was he appreciated for his incredible architecture. *The atomic age that never happened.*

Every aspect of the Beat Motel was to be praised.

Every room had framed photos of the rooms in the Paris Beat Hotel where the beat authors had written their historic books: the room where Burroughs finished "Naked Lunch", the room where Ginsberg wrote parts of "Kaddish", and so on. Yes, this place was incredible. Steve Lowe, as collectors go, was a well-kept secret.

Parked in front of the Beat Motel was also another amazing piece of history. According to Steve, it was the original trailer from the movie The Long, Long Trailer, directed by Vincente Minnelli, starring Lucille Ball and Desi Arnez. Steve being the genius that he was, saw fit to keep the inside of the trailer in mint and original condition, but painted its exterior a lovely shade of gold. It was a surreal vision parked in front of the motel. The minute I laid eyes on it, I was mesmerized. Without skipping a beat, I knew I had to do a photo session in the doorway of that trailer.

As we were packing our bags, I remembered the photo session and thought, Oh, I feel too fat; I'll do it the next time. Then I caught a look at myself in the mirror. Still not satisfied with the way I looked, something came over me.

Fuck it! I'm doing this.

I turned to my boyfriend and reminded him of the photo session. He was great when it came to shooting photos. He had an incredible camera, and he was ready to do it in minutes. So was I, seeing how I didn't need much clothes for the shot. Come to think of it, I was already dressed for the shot, or rather, undressed.

Dressed in a black bra and panties, I threw on some black spiked stilettos and wrapped my pale white frame in a white terry cloth robe, and we ran down to the trailer. As I was posing for the shots, my shameless and unabashed photographer suggested that I take *all* my clothes off. "All of them?" "Yes Iris, all of them. Take your clothes off!" He demanded. But we were right on the main highway, Hacienda Avenue. Where there was a constant flow of traffic. And I just thought, fuck it, why not? I've never been naked in public. It's not like I was sleepwalking, stark raving mad, or drunk and in a blackout. I was wide-awake, completely sober, with three cups of coffee in me, and I was fully aware of what I was about to do. Then I thought to myself, I'm a grown woman. I can take my clothes off—in the middle of the day, outdoors, in public on a main highway in the center of town—if I want to. What's the worst thing that could happen? I could get arrested? I could see it now. My celly would ask, "So, what are you in for?" I'd calmly reply, "Being naked on Hacienda Avenue." It had a nice ring to it.

And the next thing I know, I'm standing right there, in front of God and the Devil and everyone in between, stark naked in black, spike stilettos on Hacienda Avenue.

This was a golden moment, a pin-up moment, for all of Desert Hot Springs to see. In broad fucking daylight. A real live naked pin-up girl posing cheesecake in the doorway of the golden "Long, Long Trailer" grasping an old typewriter like a long lost lover.

There was something very visceral about it. The hot desert wind blowing across my pale white skin. Cars were honking, people were shouting and gawking and screaming, brakes were screeching to a halt.

Cars could be wrecked, I thought.

Part of me said no, but another, more primal part of me thought yes...

Let the whole world explode because I'm standing naked in the road...

* * *

Twenty days after the photo shoot, Steve Lowe was rushed to the hospital and died of a heart attack at the age of fifty-six. Sadly, the Beat Motel closed its bohemian doors on January 20, 2007. A sad and tragic loss for us all.

Steve Lowe, may you rest in peace...

Thank You From The Bottom of My Purse

How many times can a girl clean out her purse…

In my lifetime, it's probably been close to a million.

You can tell a lot about a person

by what's inside their purse

the condition of it

whether it's clean, messy, or cluttered

items needed and unneeded—sentimental, or kept by guilt.

My purse has black hair ties

hair clips, press-on nails

sun glasses

an iPhone, eyeliner, mascara

natural beige Revlon foundation

with sunblock,

stolen pens,

Dodger ticket stubs,

a Mexican wrestling backstage pass

stray sequins

boa feathers

Revlon's Cherries In The Snow lipstick

or Color Frost Sunsonic

candy of some variation

phone numbers on napkins—from I don't know who

Marlboro Lights in the box

a wallet that acts like a slinky

and keys to five different houses that aren't mine

and two business that aren't mine either

to places I don't know where they belong to anymore.

I like to change my wallet

every time my life goes into a new phase.

Funny, this last phase,

 I didn't change my wallet; I forgot.

The phase was so goddamn traumatic

and it just kept coming on like a tsunami

a traunami

as I like to call it

one heartbreak after the next

Car wrecks

people turning, throwing fits and chairs

losing their life savings and minds

cousins blowing brains out

In the course of one year

I've moved three times

and I still don't feel like I live anywhere.

After a while, I just want all my things in one place

The first move was to the beach at Christmas time

I knew it was a bad idea. I had my own place

but we were going to get married

and the view of the ocean was right out my window

Then the landlord passed on in April

so we moved to Atwater

built our two-story dream home

and didn't make it through a remodel

one neck surgery

too much debt

and the fear of being vulnerable

A lot of my very important things

are still in the trunk of my car

or his house

because I have nowhere to put them

or they're lost forever

Staying with family

It was supposed to be temporary

but things happen

global financial unrest

Job's shrink

and expand and shrink again

or disappear and mom's get sick

and I can't and won't leave

It's *Hotel California*

or just some vortex

that I'm right where I'm supposed to be

Don't get me wrong

I have a roof over my head

it's my heart that feels homeless

I've watched too many things go sour

too many people go south and turn on a dime

and I ask myself

Is it the economy

 Is it you

Is it me

As I'm digging through my purse

for the one millionth time

and I forget what I'm looking for...

Loan Sharks and Stolen Hearts

I remember how you sat by my bedside

that time I was in the hospital

and you spent the night

It was the most time

we ever spent together

I was 17

going under the knife

and I watched you

watch me

sign papers

that stated

results of surgery

may cause infertility

you looked so worried

I'd never seen you like that

I was shocked

you, always so bullet proof

and the super hero

never showing any worry

needs or pain

and never complained

or said a bad word

about mom

they way she did

about you...

you even scolded me once

for being mad at her

and you never scolded me.

Others spent more time with you

because of my mother's disdain

and for that

I was jealous

after hearing all the great stories from cousins

how wonderful you were

and how generous

and how much they loved you

like you were some kind of

rock god

or movie star

and of course they always threw in,

"and oh, Iris, he loves you so much."

But that never helped

yes, it was lovely to know

I always knew

I just rarely got to feel

love from a distance

is like shooting bad dope

waiting for a rush

that never comes…

I don't blame you

I don't know who to blame

it wouldn't matter anyway

there are some emotional debts

that can never be repaid

I'm just glad we got to spend

that time together

It meant a lot to me…

I know how much you hated hospitals.

THE END

About the Author –

Iris Berry is a native Angelino and one of the true and original progenitors of the L.A. punk scene. She's spent her lifetime in the city of angels producing over three decades worth of prose, poetry, and spoken word. She is one of the founding creative minds behind Punk Hostage Press. Internationally known, her wit and often dark, factual accuracy and empathy for her subjects has brought critical acclaim as well as a huge fan base. She is the author of several books including "Two Blocks East of Vine," "The Daughters of Bastards," and "The Underground Guide to Los Angeles." Berry has appeared in numerous films, TV commercials, documentaries, and iconic rock videos. In the 1980s she was a singer for the punk band the Lame Flames. Later Berry co-founded The Ringling Sisters, who recorded with legendary producer Lou Adler (A&M Records). Berry also sang and wrote songs and recorded with the Dickies, the Flesh Eaters and Pink Sabbath. She's received two certificates of merit and achievement from the city of Los Angeles for her contribution as a Los Angeles writer, and for her extensive charity work. She served four years on the Board of Directors for Beyond Baroque Literary/Arts Center. Berry has served as the mentor to many up and coming writers. With her prolific creative output, devoted work ethic, and passionate artistic integrity and social awareness, Iris has been an inspiration to generations of writers and artists of Los Angeles.

Photo by Christopher Martin

More about the Author and the Book –

"Iris Berry's frank and touching effort, The Daughters of Bastards, brings the radiant beauty of her poetic voice to the strange, funny, grotesque and poignant events of a life lived in extremes, a journey to the end of night that ends with the break of luminous day."

Richard Modiano –
Director of Beyond Baroque Literary Arts Center

"Iris Berry has no choice but to give witness. The universe ordained it with her birthplace and time and her path from there… the white chick from Pacoima with a hard edge and soft heart, the obedient princess reporting observances of special climates at guarded campfires, whose journey spanned regions most others can only dream of. Iris is the only L.A. punk diva that survived the time's brutal but privileged initiations; from sitting shotgun on suburban rides to sitting at her throne in the tinsel town underground with "the tick tick ticking" of her celluloid memory, saving it all for later, for her precision finesse in story telling… there is no other writer's witness that is as crucial to this city's history during its sexiest defiance, the punk rock Hollywood scene, as seen and transposed by a humble diva whose honesty reflects her deeply felt experiences told in a pure raw beauty of expression, weaving a noir that only Iris has lived through and here shares with us until we sweat glitter, guitars, needles and leopard skin. And we marvel at her success in never losing that sexy sweetness only a true punk princess is born with: an unconditional love and compassion for all things outside of the box."

Yvonne De la Vega – Los Angeles poet/organizer - World Poetry Movement. Author of "Tomorrow, Yvonne – Poetry & Prose For Suicidal Egotists"

"There are far too few writers today who write from the heart about the damned. Far too few who let lost souls scream from the page once more. Iris Berry is one of these writers. Her words are haunting and her imagery cinematic. Iris Berry is a straight Razor wrapped in a garter belt. She leaves nothing but her blood on the page. The writing community should consider itself lucky to have such a talent. The Daughters of Bastards proves this beauty is a beast of a writer…."

James Trompeano III- Author of Gutterfish-Chandler Circle Press, The Thorazine Hotel-Unadorned Press, and The Red Hook Giraffe- Punk Hostage Press (2016)

"I will not speak in cliché about Iris Berry, nor will I use unnecessary superlatives. When I think of this artist I think of enchantment and beauty. I think of intelligence and perspicacity. Iris is one fine talent honed by life and all the better for it. She writes with grace and strength and allows you to live the moments she creates so that you not only wish you were there with her to experience life as she beholds it but for all intents you are there experiencing the ragged emotion and reality that makes an Iris Berry work come to life."

Larry Jaffe – Poet

MORE PUNK HOSTAGE PRESS BOOKS

FRACTURED (2012) by Danny Baker

BETTER THAN A GUN IN A KNIFE FIGHT (2012) by A. Razor
DRAWN BLOOD: COLLECTED WORKS FROM D.B.P.LTD., 1985-1995 (2012) by A. Razor
BEATEN UP BEATEN DOWN (2012) by A. Razor
SMALL CATASTROPHES IN A BIG WORLD (2012) by A. Razor
HALF-CENTURY STATUS (2013) by A. Razor
DAYS OF XMAS POEMS (2014) by A. Razor

IMPRESS (2012) by C.V. Candi V. Auchterlonie

TOMORROW, YVONNE - POETRY & PROSE FOR SUICIDAL EGOISTS (2012) by Yvonne De la Vega

MIRACLES OF THE BLOG: A SERIES (2012) by Carolyn Srygley-Moore

8TH & AGONY (2012) by Rich Ferguson

UNTAMED (2013) by Jack Grisham

CODE BLUE: A LOVE STORY (2014) by Jack Grisham

MOTH WING TEA (2013) by Dennis Cruz
THE BEAST IS WE (2018) by Dennis Cruz

SHOWGIRL CONFIDENTIAL (2013) by Pleasant Gehman

DREAMS GONE MAD WITH HOPE (2014) by S.A. Griffin

HOW TO TAKE A BULLET AND OTHER SURVIVAL POEMS (2014) by Hollie Hardy

MORE PUNK HOSTAGE PRESS BOOKS

YEAH, WELL... (2014) by Joel Landmine

DEAD LIONS (2014) by A.D. Winans

SCARS (2014) by Nadia Bruce Rawlings

STEALING THE MIDNIGHT FROM A HANDFUL OF
DAYS (2014) by Michele McDannold

WHEN I WAS A DYNAMITER, Or, How a Nice Catholic
Boy Became a Merry Prankster, a Pornographer, and a
Bridegroom Seven Times (2104) by Lee Quarnstrom

I WILL ALWAYS BE YOUR WHORE/LOVE SONGS for
Billy Corgan (2014) by Alexandra Naughton

YOU COULD NEVER OBJECTIFY ME MORE THAN I'VE
ALREADY OBJECTIFIED MYSELF (2015) by Alexandra
Naughton

INTROVERT/EXTROVERT (2015) by Russell Jaffe

NO PARACHUTES TO CARRY ME HOME (2015)
by Maisha Z Johnson

#1 SON AND OTHER STORIES (2017)
by Michael Marcus

LOOKING FOR JOHNNY, THE LEGEND OF JOHNNY
THUNDERS by Danny Garcia (2018)

THE BEAS IS WE by Dennis Cruz (2018)

ALL THAT SHINES UNDER THE HOLLYWOOD SIGN
by Iris Berry (2019).

Made in the USA
San Bernardino, CA
07 July 2020